I0151353

TRUE CONFESSIONS

poems by

Joanne Greenway

Finishing Line Press
Georgetown, Kentucky

TRUE CONFESSIONS

*For all the Sabareses, Pontecorvos, Confortis
and Schiavos for making the journey
that led to mine.*

ACKNOWLEDGMENTS

My sincere thanks to the poets of the Greater Cincinnati Writers League for
their wisdom and support over the years. They have made me a better poet
and a better person.

Publisher: Leah Maines

Editor: Christen Kincaid

Cover Art: *The Temptation of Eve,* by sculptor Gislebertus
          Photographer / copyrightholder: G. Dagli Orti.
          Licensed to: Joanne Greenway, August 1, 2019.

Author Photo: Karen Gaski

Cover Design: Elizabeth Maines McCleavy

Printed in the USA on acid-free paper.
Order online: www.finishinglinepress.com
          also available on amazon.com

Author inquiries and mail orders:
Finishing Line Press
P. O. Box 1626
Georgetown, Kentucky 40324
U. S. A.

Table of Contents

THE DIXIE CUP CURE

A stroke of packaging
genius. Ice cream in neat,
single servings, with little
paper-wrapped wooden
spoons. Pull off the lid and
on the underside, smiling
through a milky film, find
your favorite Hollywood star:
Clark Gable, Betty Grable,
Roy and Ginger Rogers.

My mother could cure a sore
throat with a chocolate Dixie Cup.
Even now, when the mercury
dips and the hawk howls,
I crave the cold comfort
of ice cream, loaded with
butterfat. Just one mouthful,
enough to bring back a time
when life tasted sweeter
and I was deserving of love.

THE LITTLE QUEEN OF CLEAN

Mommy says it's a Bissell's Little Queen,
a child-size carpet sweeper, to school me
in how to care for that split-level Cape
I will keep tidy for my future husband.
An unwelcome Christmas present, a marvel
in maroon and blue plastic. Rotating twin
brushes to make child's play of housework.

Bissell's Little Queen was a drag with
no talent for picking up dirt. I fight all day
with my brother over what I really covet—
his train set. He got to have all the fun
while I learned from mother how to iron
dish towels, sheets and pillowcases.
Bless June Cleaver's Immaculate Heart.
She never sweated off her make-up
swabbing floors in her pristine shirtwaist.

Forgive me, Mother, it has been decades
since my last confession. I am guilty
of the sin of sloth. I own three seldom-used
vacuum cleaners. I have learned to co-exist
with clutter. If cleanliness is next to godliness,
I am irredeemable. This shameless sloven
sits in her living room, awaiting damnation
while dust motes dance in afternoon sun.

ABLUTIONS

Make-up artists could never duplicate
that pearlescent glow. My mother's face
might have been the model for my favorite
doll—rosy cheeked, perfect bisque head.
Pond's Cold Cream was all she ever used.
Laid on thick, then tissued off until even
her vivid Hazel Bishop lipstick vanished.

There were separate taps for hot and cold
on our ancient hand sink. She would fill
her cupped hands first with cold, then hot.
Again and again she carried the water
to her face—a purification rite she reveled
in, soothing as the waters of Lethe. Then
she would gently pat her face dry. *Never
rub or pull your skin,* she had warned.
Use moisturizer every night before bed.

Hers was by Avon, sold door-to-door
by a colored lady. When Clara visited,
she left behind tiny sample lipsticks—
little gold bullets I pilfered for my own
stealth make-up sessions. All I wanted
was to be as beautiful as my mother.

When she died at eighty-two, her face was
still as luminous as her glow-in-the-dark
statue of the Virgin Mary. I would petition
Mary to look after my immaculate mother
in Heaven—full of grace and fair of face.
I still hold in my heart the dewy warmth
of her soft, smooth cheek against mine.

WHAT YOU LEFT BEHIND

You kept every book you ever read,
every term paper you ever wrote,
even some yellowed grade school
report cards—mostly As, a few Bs.

Once, in what you would have called
a "rare burst of domesticity," I pitched
all your books and papers—except one,
the first draft of your dissertation: *Tense,
Aspect and Mood in Modern German.*

I understood precious little of this
scholarly work, but never considered
consigning it to the recycling bin.
Like a bone fragment from a martyred
saint, it is preserved and revered,
on the top shelf of the bookcase.

What was so fascinating to you
is as much a mystery to me as
its erudite, inscrutable author.
I never read beyond the first page.

I never got to the end of you, either.

CHUBBETTES AD, 1956

Your chubby lass can be the belle
of her class, it read. Except the child
model in the ad was not chubby,
by anyone's standards.

I hated the Chubbettes brand
as much as I hated my body.
My mother moved buttons
opened darts, added gussets—
while I holed up in my room,
studying *Seventeen* magazine:
page after page of sweet-faced
teen models, all scrubbed,
perfectly made-up, wearing
clothes way too fussy
and formal for everyday.
Still, I would have sold
my own mother up the river
for a junior petite body
and a *Seventeen* wardrobe.

For the message was clear—
nothing mattered in life
as much as how you looked.
But Chubbettes insisted,
She can have a tummy
and still look yummy!
Did I mention their penchant
for cheap shots in cheap rhyme?

Over the years, I tried
Overeaters Anonymous,
Jack LaLanne, Weight Watchers,
Jazzercise, Jane Fonda, Pritikin,
South Beach, Atkins, amphetamines—
each sortie into self-improvement
deserted in favor of dessert.

Then came the epiphany—
starve no longer for approval.
Whet your appetite for bliss.

THE PIE WAR

Hunger had been his familiar. Fortune smiled
when he found my mother, a woman born
to love and nurture, a woman who learned
to bake, just to sate his tyrant sweet tooth.

For fifteen years, unabated sweetness—
then along came Lucy—unhappy wife
of an older man, now just an old man.
Lucy had a cloud of auburn hair,
a saucy manner and quick Irish wit.
She visited a lot, never empty-handed.
Used to bring us pies and such, sparking
a tacit baking rivalry with my mother
whose own fruit pies were peerless.

Baking was not Lucy's forte. Many
fine pie apples perished ignobly
in her pies—entombed in fatty crusts,
cooked to a sweet and gluey mush.

My class act mother refused to react
while Lucy flirted with my father right
in front of her at our kitchen table.
Wearing an indulgent smile, she served
up the coffee and the dreadful pie,
silently wishing they'd gag on it—
while charming, chatty Lucy convinced
my Dad he'd hung the moon and stars.

He ate it all up. And the bad pie, too.

INDOOR CAT'S LAMENT

Do-gooder cat wranglers brought me
to this shelter, then sold me to you
for sixty bucks and a solemn promise
that I would live out all my nine lives
under house arrest. Humane? Not!

It was a guilt-driven move: you needed
a companion for The Other Cat. Bah!
It is not company she craves, but deep
REM sleep. She is the fabled feline
frequently mistaken for a meatloaf.

Outside, rabbits ravage your garden.
I sit on the sill watching, powerless.
The Other Cat lazes and lolls all day,
no catly curiosity of the world outside.
I am dying to snuff just one baby bunny…

The Other Cat, a furry, black spheroid,
ignores me. Refuses to join me in play.
But let Fatty find a paperclip on the floor,
and she erupts in paroxysms of joy.
How stupid are some cats? Sad!

In my dreams, I live in Ancient Egypt:
a regal, revered Cat God whose followers
leave offerings of meat, milk and spices
in my temple. I wear earrings, a jeweled
collar and have my run of the desert.

I cannot guarantee I won't attack your
fleshy ankles out of sheer frustration.
Even human felons get a furlough!
Where is my stash of kitty reefer?
I am jonesing for some high-grade 'nip.

ARTIFACTS

I have watched many pieces
of your life walk out the door:
the Korg electric piano, some
lightly-used power tools.
Boxes of books: Greek and Latin
grammars, linguistics texts by
Chomsky, Cline and Korsakov.
Piles of old class notes and
academic papers, all bound
in blue folders, labeled
in your neat, blocky script.
Clothing, shoes and golf clubs—
all of it boxed up for Goodwill.

The green Eddie Bauer jacket stayed.
It was so like you: Gortex-tough shell,
sturdy and substantial, so many pockets,
inside and out, some hidden. So practical,
with all the snaps and a two-way zipper.
Set me back three bills.

You only wore it snow-blowing
the driveway. After twenty minutes,
it made you sweat like a stevedore.
You asked if you could re-gift it
to your brother. I laid on the guilt.

After you died, I kept it another
ten years. Magical thinking decreed
you would wear it again when you
came back. I would open the hall
closet door, take in a faint whiff
of cedar, and there you'd be:
your green jacket crusted with snow,
tiny icicles clinging to your beard,
your face burnished a healthy pink.

You would thank me again
for never letting you feel the cold.

GHOST LULLABY

My father once told me I looked
just like her. There was proof
in an old, photograph. Across
six decades, my grandmother gazes
at me through tired, inkwell eyes.
The faint smile cannot hide her
melancholy. She died young,
leaving behind one angry man,
twenty acres of fruit trees and
five children she could no longer
shield from their father's wrath.

The old man drank as hard as he
worked. Get in the way of those
heavy hands at your peril. Deep
in the orchard, she made the bootleg
whiskey that quenched his rage.

I wish I had memories of nesting
in her lap as she sang me to sleep:
Ninna nanna, ninna oh
*Questo bimbo a chi lo dò?**
I see her kissing my dimpled
little fist, her face lighting up
when I tender the hint of a smile.

Forever absent, I can only
conjure the sound of her voice,
the yeasty scent of her clothes,
the savor of her sweet moonshine.

*TRANSLATION
Lullaby, lullaby, ooh,
Who will I give this baby to?

TESTIMONIAL OF THE CHRONICALLY
ENABLED, OR WTF?

This poem drew inspiration from a Facebook post
by Sandra Hempel, who died in October, 2016,
leaving this world far too soon.

Her last MRI really was her last MRI.
The tumor was back, boring into her brain
jelly like a carpenter bee. She takes her laptop
to bed and hits the keys with purpose:

For the rest of my life, I will never…
Suffer another root canal.
Sit through pointless meetings.
Shave my legs.
Endure mammograms.
Count carbs and calories.
Scoop Pongo's poop.
Rake leaves in the autumn wind.
Face down five loads of laundry.
Worry about my bank balance.

Forget the bucket list. No time.
I give you instead, my fuck it list:
For the rest of my life, I will…
Wear sweat pants all day, every day.
Swear off bras with underwire cups.
Eat as much bacon as I want.
Order a bunch of crap from Amazon.
Watch bad reality TV all day long.
Pop Percocet and Valium like m&ms.
Share my bed with the dog.
Huddle close with my besties.
Embarrass my young children,
pulling them close, dandling them
on my lap like babies, holding tight.

God is on their shit-list right now—
they are even angry at me. One day,
they will remember their mother
as a fierce Freyja, dueling toe-to-toe
with the Angel of Death. The mother
who refused to go down easy. So strong,
so stubborn, they had to bury her standing.

WAKE UP CALL

Contra vim Veneris
herbam non inveneris;
contra vim mortis non
crescit herba in hortis

Neither din of rush hour nor drone
of lawn mower is enough to muffle
the top-note of the mourning dove.
In three forlorn cries, an impatient
male urges his mate back to the nest.
Come home. Come home. Coo-woo.

To the bereft, their message is:
Grieve not; your dear ones
are close. Pay attention. Believe.
I refuse to be consoled by this
muted, melancholy earworm
playing in my head all day long,

the head of a mud-bound woman who
shuns the so-called sweet hereafter.
Feathered couriers from the spirit world
are no comfort to me. I want heaven
here on Earth—to root and grow where
I am planted and compost to soil;

soil that will spawn seeds and snails
enough to feed an entire flock.
May it grow herbs strong enough
to cure Love, to cure Death. Strong
enough to quell the clarion call
of the dolorous mourning dove.

TRANSLATION: *Against the strength of love,*
                      you will find no herb.
                      Against the strength of death,
                      no herb grows in the garden

11

GRATITUDE

He would have no truck with the sacraments
and saints of the Catholic Church. It was
The Wheel he worshiped in his cinderblock
tabernacle. The hum of a well-tuned engine
was a mantra for my ace mechanic father.

Back in the Fifties, our New York hamlet
was a haven for mob guys flying under
the radar. One summer, Sally "the Zip"
Testa drove up from the City, maddened
by an automotive mystery: a persistent
rattle in his brand new '57 Mercury
Turnpike Cruiser. No garage or dealership
had succeeded in silencing that annoying
noise. At the urging of Bambi, owner
of the town's one and only gin mill, Sally
brought his showboat to my father's shop.

In short order, Dad found the culprit:
a loose bolt where the torque converter
joined the flywheel, an assembly line
error. It was an easy fix for my Dad,
a man fluent in the language of cars.
Pop became Sally's *goomba* on the spot.

Where Sally ranked in the mob chain
of command—"made" guy, capo or
soldier—was unclear. We just knew,
while my father was greasing cars,
Sally was greasing his boss's enemies.
Omertà made good business sense.

One thing about wise guys, they never
forget a favor. For decades afterward,
whenever Sally came to town, Dad never
paid for another drink at Bambi's Bar.

BOOK CLUB SMACKDOWN

Sarah scoffs at Terri's book choice.
Brands it brain candy. Good beach
reading, but hardly good fiction.
Hyper-educated, upper-crusty Brit,
Sarah loves to flaunt her high-brow
literary taste. I play Switzerland
but secretly long for a Brexit.

Judith opines we are reading too many
downer books. Proposes *Strangers
in Their Own Land,* a book meant
to help us understand Trump voters.
Talk about your downers, wisecracks
Opal, our well-oiled Southern sass-box.
She drains her wine glass, urges us
to bring copies to the next meeting
—so we can burn them.

Pamela, our lone Independent, pushes
for some escapist fare. I just know
she reads bodice-rippers on the sly.
Mazie blames the Merlot, suggests any
Alexander McCall Smith novel;
palatable, apolitical fare, laced
with Scottish drollery. Luci labels it
literary flotsam. Take out all the filler
and his pap would fit on a postcard.

We are deadlocked, desperately in need
of a shaman to herd us into a sweat lodge
and leave us 'til we purge our prejudices.
I think of quitting the group—again
—until I realize my only social
outlet is this monthly literary tilt
with a roomful of bibulous book lovers.

I am going to need more wine.

TRUE CONFESSIONS

Lapsed Catholic I may be, but
I still invoke St. Anthony when
I lose something: *Tony, Tony,
look around. See if my car keys
can be found.* Damned if it doesn't
work every time. I am afflicted
with a sort of Catholic Tourette's
that makes me write "Sending prayers"
in sympathy cards or, worse yet,
"He's in a better place." I invoke
the Almighty whenever someone
sneezes—quickly! Before Satan
can breach open nasal passages.

Confession was not good for my soul.
As a child of eight, I sinned by fibbing
about the nature and number of my sins.
compounding my venial sin count.
I was absolved with an Act of Contrition
and puny penance. Ten Hail Marys,
and I was good to go until the next
occasion for sin. As a matter of taste,
I never confessed my impure thoughts.

My career as a doubter launched early
with *My First Book of Bible Stories.*
It told how it took Our Lord only
seven days to create heaven and earth.
Roughly the same amount of time
it takes to get through airport security.
And what about that pretty, full-color
illustration of Adam and Eve gamboling
in the Garden—with belly buttons…

My passive-aggressive piety forced me
to feign belief in a God who lets bad
stuff happen to good people. Even
if you pray so hard, you get rope burn
from your rosary, floods, forest fires,
tsunamis and suicide bombings—
shit is still gonna happen.

It's all on the good Lord's to-do list.

GOOD TO GO

In my dream, the Grim Reaper appears,
in Bermuda shorts. It is July, after all,
so he is dressed for the weather. He bears
in his bony arms his trademarked scythe,
a plate heaped high with greasy French fries
and a cheeseburger in a little Styrofoam casket.

I try to explain I only eat fries once a month,
shun coconut oil, trans and saturated fat.
Even so, I wonder if I can really add more
years of life by forgoing a pile of fried
potatoes, glistening with fat, showered
with salt. Will I suffer divine retribution
for indulging in one of life's great pleasures?
May lightning strike me down—
near an emergency room—if my gamble
does not pay off. I am playing fat gram
roulette, hoping the Statin drug dose
that gives me nocturnal leg cramps and
robs me of sleep will spare me the agony
of a heart attack. Thrice weekly trips
to the gym make me feel virtuous,
but the wiry young woman keeping
a blazing pace one treadmill over reminds
me how elusive my fitness goals are.

I just want to lose just enough weight
so I can cross my legs in hot weather.
I count carbs like coins from my purse,
defying the doom of diabetes. I joined
the gym to break a sweat three times
a week, but the treadmill bores me.
I weigh myself before heading to my locker.
The numbers are the same. Driving home,
the Reaper rides shotgun. Steak n' Shake
beckons… Who wants to live forever?

HANGY PANTS

Two weeks after his sudden death
she cleans out his pick-up and learns
what killed him—stashed in the console,
a trove of candy bars and little white pills.

What kills her is his text message trail.
Moony missives from his slice on the side,
the back-burner babe who had kept him
company when he worked out of town.

On a sunny, windless summer day, she fires up
the grill and carries out a second cremation.
The laundry hamper still held the odor of his
human mush: sweaty work clothes, golf togs.

She makes a suttee of each sock and shirt.
All her illusions wither in curls of ash;
plumes of acrid smoke climb skyward,
leaving nothing but soot and sorrow.

Back in their favorite diner, she recoils
at the smell of burnt coffee and lies.
Fluorescent lights flicker and buzz—
the Muzak of a dream dying hard.

THE CHILDREN TELL OF WAR

René
lost a finger during
the Nazi occupation.
A child resistance fighter
now past 80, a souvenir
of his courage remains,
always at arm's length.

Bette's Delft-blue eyes
shimmer with tears
when she tells
how her parents
kept from starving.
They dug up every
tulip bulb they could find.

Saul, the salesman,
works with sleeves rolled up,
exposing his left forearm.
He must have been around
six when they stamped him.
I am struck mute with rage.
Puzzled, he asks, *Are you OK?*

Karl finds an old photo
of his adored father, in uniform,
the *Hakenkreuz* emblazoned
on his sleeve. For him,
there will be no truce,
no lasting Peace, in a heart
filled with love and shame.

Marie-Cécile,
evacuated to a foster home
after the war, was starved
for food and affection. Lost all
her French except for one phrase:
On m'a laissée toute seule.
You left me all alone.

BILLET DOUX

Like a moth falling to its death,
a slip of folded white paper
escapes from the pages
of Merwin's *Collected Poems*
as I browse in Half Price Books.
You are the kind of man
I've always wanted.
Have a great day, sweetheart.
Can't wait to see you again.
Love always,
Katy.

The cynical me wonders
if she read that article
in Cosmo: *One Hundred*
Tips to Keep Your Love Alive.
I picture her planting little
billets doux everywhere:
in his underwear drawer,
among his threadbare briefs;
tucked between a few bills
in his wallet; surprising him
from his shaving kit, lurking
deep in his fusty gym bag.

I begin to wonder if, like this
volume of poetry, was Katy
deep discounted and moved
to the remainder bin?
Men are like mercury:
elusive, yet dangerous to hold—
chemistry is so overrated.

One evening, home from work,
I imagine her finding a note
from him on the mantelpiece.

Dear Katy,

I am so sorry. I can't do this anymore.
It was good while it lasted. Thank you

for sweet memories of lap robes,
herbal tea and poetry.

Fondly,
Fred

P.S. Please, keep the Merwin book.

TWEETS FROM INTERSTATE 80

Road work ahead. Left lane closed. Cretin
in pick-up refuses to fall in behind me.
Races ahead, then tries to cut in.
I shall deny him three times.
#WheelsofJustice

Rest stop vending machine will not give up
my Twizzlers. Keeps the change. Anger,
highway fatigue, craving denied.
Surely a recipe for road rage.
#TWIZZLERchiseler

Amish family boards Ford Transit van.
A shabat goy drives them long distances.
Modernity embraced when convenient.
Do they not understand cheating is a sin?
#SPEEDdemons

Comfort Inn anything but comfortable.
Impossible to read. Only 40-watt bulbs
in the lamps. Impossible to sleep.
AC louder than the New York subway.
#StillBeatsFlying

Stale Danish, 30-weight coffee, I flee
the Comfort Inn. Man kneels distraught
in right lane up ahead. A black bear
has lost its battle with his F-150.
#BEARdown

Heading home, I miss my Columbus
exit. The chili dog from Cissy's Diner
will keep me awake the rest of the trip
for all the wrong reasons.
#FastFoodAcida

Home after thirteen hours on the road.
My two cats circle me, aloof and sullen.
I know this will not last. They will
feign affection for food.
#WildCatStrike

IN VINO VERITAS

The first pour:
a chewy Cab Sauv.
Great nose, even over
Graham's lime aftershave.
Ted swirls and spits
and holds forth
on tannins and tartness
Bandies terms like balance
and bite. After the third pour,
his face turns red,
his voice grows louder,
his tongue looser…
Karen hustles him out
to the parking lot
and wrestles him
for the car keys.

Carole is on the prowl.
Splashes a fine Romanée
all over Vince's white shirt.
Grabs a bar cloth and blots
him up and down
a little too thoroughly
Her feigned contrition
does not fool anyone.
Vince leaves early and alone,
to do his laundry.

Iain thought the Malbec
was over-extracted,
as flat and lifeless
as his marriage.
The haughty maître d' blows
him off. Iain would like
to argue with him, but
Sophie's lightning elbow
stops him cold.
The rest of us side with Iain,
but are too cowardly
to dump and rinse.

Sophie cannot wait
for dessert: champagne
and petits fours. Iain mocks her,
a peasant who cannot tell
Red Ripple from a Côtes du Rhone.
He is a fine Bordeaux man,
wasted on a grilled cheese woman.

COLLEGE OF CARDINALS

Marmalade the cat rivets her owlish
eyes on the cardinals flocking to my
feeder. Under house arrest for years,
she still craves the hunt. If she could,

she would scatter their crimson plumes
like rose petals at a wedding. Cardinals
are said to be our late lamented ancestors,
visiting from the spirit world. Since they are

family, I invite them in for tea and cake.
They perch on my spare wooden chairs,
blinding me with the light of their angel eyes.
I do not entirely welcome these avian envoys

from the Sweet Hereafter. I dread what
news they may bring. Marmalade, clearly
spooked, has gone into hiding. Meanwhile,
the birds peck at their cake until only crumbs

remain—they leave their tea untouched.
I ask them what it's like on the Other Side.
They answer with a furious flapping
of wings, then fly off in a heartbeat.

Feeling bereft, I watch from my window
as their paint-box red fades to black.
For a moment, their beauty was enough
to quiet the flutter of angels' wings.

IL MIO CANE CAPISCE L'ITLIANO
(My Dog Understands Italian)

The sunspot on the kitchen floor
beckons him like the warm pavestones
of a Roman piazza. Today's achievements
are many: digging like a backhoe, he turned
the yard into a moonscape in pursuit
of a single mole. Even ran off a terrorist
working undercover for FedEx. And scared
the bejesus out of two Jehovah's Witnesses.

Only hunger pangs can wake him from his
death-like slumber. This *dolce far niente*
surfs the kitchen counters, pouncing
on unattended loaves of bread, half-made
sandwiches and sticks of butter, paper
wrapper included. Despite such gluttony,
he begs shamelessly at dinnertime,
drilling me with his liquid brown eyes.

Tonight, I relent and spoil him with his
favorite: *pasta con acciughe.* His bad
breath, with its topnote of anchovy,
would knock a buzzard off a shit pile.

Bedtime. He follows me upstairs and takes
his position across the doorsill, his body
a fortress, walling off every possible threat.

I kiss his head and coo: *Buona notte, caro.*
From the dark, he answers: *Sospiro.**

* *Sospiro: "sigh" in Italian.*

THE CROW MOON

Murmuration: when
hundreds of birds,
roosting silently in trees,
rise, sudden and raucous.
Ascending all at once,
hungry for the sky,
they hover and heave,
as if knitted together,
moving in one
amorphous cloud.
Though leaderless,
they seem to know
where they're going.
No collisions,
no crash landings.
as if they inhabited
one body and one soul.

The Algonquins
hang this lunacy
on the Crow Moon—
when trees green up,
seedheads burst,
rain churns the earth
and streams swell.

The Crow Moon
is the last
winter moon,
when weary Earth
tilts its worn face
to the warming sun.

BUM STEER

Back when gas was twenty-nine cents
a gallon, our dad owned a two-pump
Esso gas station and body shop. He hauled
wrecked cars to the shop with a flashy
two-tone tow truck, painted pink and blue.

In the middle of dinner one night, a frantic
farm boy burst through our kitchen door.
One of his grandfather's cows had fallen
into a well and was sinking fast. Towing
crumpled cars was one thing, but winching
a Black Angus steer was quite another.

Without a minute's hesitation, my dad
and brother headed up the road in that pastel
tow truck. The rescue mission was a success;
they pulled the hapless bovine from his
earthen prison—and the well was sealed.
But so was his fate, for the Black Angus
breed is prized for its meat, not its milk—
no happy ending except for us carnivores.

TAG, YOU'RE IT, a Pantoum

We ran ourselves breathless on summer nights.
Distant thunder rolled like a slow-moving train.
Forks of lightning turned the sky yellow-white;
We played on, mocking the menace of the rain.

In the distance, the whistle of a low moaning train.
Under cover of darkness, pursuing each other,
We played on, heedless of the coming rain.
We played on, ignoring the pleas from our mothers.

Through the high grass, we pursued each other—
It was all about us, not the passage of time.
We played on, ignoring the pleas from our mothers.
If only we'd known there would be no rewind.

We were giddy at play, heedless of risk or reason.
The road ahead stretched endless, smooth and long.
No one told us childhood was but a single season,
Or we might have paused to savor our song.

We ran ourselves breathless on summer nights,
Our playground churned to mud by a roaring downpour.
Thunder boom and lightning flash filled us with fright,
Sent us fleeing like thieves, scrambling for the door.

VITO'S GIFT

I read to my literary mother from a dusty
anthology while she cooks our dinner. Mostly
classic stuff: Burns, Teasdale, Whitman,
Longfellow and Poe. Vito, an old *paisano*

fond of books, even fonder of my mother,
had given her this tattered tome. The only
thing Dad ever read was *Popular Mechanics*.
I stop reading when he comes in, his hands

scrubbed raw, smelling of Lava soap. I bolt
out of his chair, set the table for dinner,
always at 5:30. His obsidian eyes fall
upon my book. Grandpa had started him

behind the horse and plow at age three.
Reading for pleasure only happened
in the one room school up the road,
the one he had to leave after sixth grade.

I am stunned when his lips part and spill
the words of John Greenleaf Whittier:
For of all sad words of tongue or pen,
The saddest are these: 'It might have been!'

Just one couplet was enough to remind
me I was also my father's daughter.

FATHER IS DIVINE

"Peace, it's wonderful!"   *–Father Divine*

God could get lost in a crowd in the person
of a little colored man. Did you know the Almighty
sported a perfect pencil moustache and custom
tailored suit? He said he was God. Period. Not
the Son of God or an angel sent by God. No, no.
He was God Himself. Good Christians called it
blasphemy. Others swore the gaze from his dark
eyes drilled deep down into their very souls.
They were in the presence of God, damn it.

Father Divine had taken no vow of poverty;
his Peace Mission brought in barrels of cash.
Legions joined his multi-racial Utopia and lived
on a big farm up in Ulster County. He must have
bought it through a white proxy; not many Negroes
owned land back then. It galled some folks to see
him cruising around in his Cadillac limousine.
A silver-tongued Svengali, he reeled them in
with charisma and claptrap, coining new words
along the way. Though they strove mightily,
scandal-mongers never could bring him down.

The cornerstones of his kingdom meant renouncing
welfare, credit, life insurance, tobacco, gambling,
and alcohol. Marriage was permitted, but no sex.
Rumor had it that Father allowed himself
wiggle room on the celibacy dictum. Only one
temptation of the flesh was allowed: eating. Just as
Jesus did, Father Divine fed thousands of followers
in the splendor of his sylvan estates, his "heavens"
on earth. Even during the Great Depression,
none of Father's faithful ever went hungry.

Father shed his mortal coil decades ago. His
remaining followers are steadfast in their belief
that he never died and refuse to speak of him
in the past tense. In the dining hall of their
Woodmont heaven, just outside Philly,
they continue to set a place for Him at the table.

Been waiting on the Resurrection since 1965.

STORM DAMAGE

The air tastes like metal right before leaden
clouds unleash hailstones and ropes of rain.
In my fishbowl house, one room deep, rain
has me surrounded. Water overwhelms

the paltry gutters, washing away mulch
and carving runnels into flowerbeds.
Thunder rattles the windows and my nerves.
The nest in the eaves of the front porch

may not survive. After the storm, the air
smells like mud and leaf rot. A stubborn
sun knifes through the gloom. Eerie light
reveals ruin: tattered trees, tangled flags,

toppled nests. Broken-hearted birds
squall over bits of blue on the sidewalk.

ANTIGUA HE COME FROM

A sleek, bottle-green Volvo pulls over for us.
Volvos are *the* St. Thomas status car. The driver
might be a celebrity. In the rear-view mirror,
we catch a wink and a 600-watt smile.
We squeeze into the back seat. He jokes:
Look like next time, I need a biggah cahr.

By the time he drops us off, our chauffeur
has told us he is King Obstinate, unknown
State-side, but regionally famous calypso
and *soca* singer. A shameless shill, he urges
us to catch his act in downtown Charlotte.

The club is illuminated only by candles
and stage lights glaring flame tree red.
As dark as it is, we still stand out,
the only pinkies in the joint. There
is enough *ganja* in the air to give us
a contact buzz. The music starts—
for a comely Trinidadian stripper.
We might be in the wrong club.

Without warning or introduction,
Obstinate bursts onstage, flailing
an acoustic guitar, his voice a meld
of smoke and sandpaper. He rips
through a raunchy repertoire. Our
brawny Volvo-driving teddy bear
must be a *loup garou* in the guise
of an X-rated West Indian Elvis:
a pelvis-pumping, groin-grinding,
guitar-pounding hell-raiser!

Decades later, Google unmasks him
as Paul Richards, the hotel dishwasher
who rose to hotel headliner. We reunite
on Spotify. Like Proust's *madeleine*,
he sings me back to muggy nights
on St. Thomas—rum punch sweating
my glass, *soca* soundtrack thumping,
the scarlet sun falling into the sea.

AT THE OLD GRANGE HALL, a Villanelle

We danced up a storm at the old grange hall,
metal taps on our shoes drumming the floor,
stomping and sliding to Bill's rhythmic call.

Possessed by the music, our frenzied footfall,
set skirts to swirling and our spirits to soar.
We raised the roof at that old grange hall.

Hoofing and hooting, we had us a ball.
You begged for a break, but I wanted more,
skipping and skating to Bill's rhythmic call.

No sitting one out or hugging the wall,
not while the fiddle played right to my core.
Man, we wore the boards bare at the old grange hall.

Swing that purty lil' gal, now shuffle y'all,
do-si-do and circle left around the floor,
swinging and stepping to Bill's rhythmic call.

These creaky old legs can't do much anymore;
the music seems muffled, not clear like before.
But, by damn, we were stars at the old grange hall,
setting the floor on fire to Bill's rhythmic call.

BREAKFAST AT DENNY'S

Denny's menu would
break a cardiologist's heart.
But this breakfast will power
me through the endless drive
across Pennsylvania via I-80.
A coffee carafe-wielding waitress
appears at my table, glances
at my haggard face. She knows
enough to leave the entire pot.

I perk up when two wiry, tanned
truckers stride in. One sports
a ponytail and a worn George Jones
tee shirt. They settle into the booth
in front of me unaware a shameless,
eavesdropping poet lurks nearby.

Ponytail confides to his buddy
that things are getting worse at home.
His old lady is always riding his dick
about something. It doesn't help
that he's on the road so much. Even
their mattress is a mine field. The only
thing that keeps him from walking
out—for good, this time—is their son.

The other guy adjusts his bill cap. An
over-the-road Doctor Ruth, he answers
with a question: *Do you still love her?*
Ponytail admits the heat is off. But,
if he leaves, she might keep him
from their son. That's why we have
lawyers, Bill Cap asserts. *You got rights!*

The waitress delivers their order:
two lumberjack specials, enough
to feed a Third World nation. For me,
this tale of woe will be a cliff-hanger.
Strictly none of my business, but I want
to know how this domestic drama ends.
I am invested and more pissed off

than I have a right to be. Like most
women, I always insist on closure.

They are right behind me as I wait
in line to pay my tab. As if on cue:
a bittersweet George and Tammy
duet plays over the sound system:
After the Fire Is Gone.

Joanne Greenway was born and raised in a farming community in Ulster County, New York. She holds a Master's Degree in French Literature from Indiana University (1971), but spent the bulk of her working life at Hamilton County Department of Job and Family Services, in Cincinnati. During her thirty-year career with that agency she held a variety of positions, including five years in the area of child welfare.

For the past 47 years, she has made Cincinnati her home and, in 2006, became a member of the Greater Cincinnati Writers League, a poetry organization founded in November of 1930. It is believed to be the oldest, continuously meeting poetry organization in the country. Since September of 2016, she has had the privilege of serving as president of this critique group.

True Confessions is her second published chapbook. Previously, she has been published online and in several local publications. Much of her poetry draws on recent and recovered memories of small town life and growing up in a colorful Italian-American family. When not writing, she is reading: fiction, biography and poetry. Among her many other interests: volunteering with disadvantaged elementary school children in the inner city, politics, pets and the creative and performing arts.